Inspiration

Harnessing The Power Of Inspiration For True Greatness

By Ace McCloud
Copyright © 2014

Disclaimer

The information provided in this book is designed to provide helpful information on the subjects discussed. This book is not meant to be used, nor should it be used, to diagnose or treat any medical condition. For diagnosis or treatment of any medical problem, consult your own physician. The publisher and author are not responsible for any specific health or allergy needs that may require medical supervision and are not liable for any damages or negative consequences from any treatment, action, application or preparation, to any person reading or following the information in this book. Any references included are provided for informational purposes only. Readers should be aware that any websites or links listed in this book may change.

Table Of Contents

Introduction 6
Chapter 1: An Overview of Inspiration 8
Chapter 2: The Power of Why 10
Chapter 3: Inspirational Habits 12
Chapter 4: Inspiring People/Stories 17
Chapter 5: Your Inspirational Action Plan 20
Chapter 6: Inspirational Quotes 25
Conclusion..28
My Other Books and Audio Books.............................29

Be sure to check out my website for all my Books and Audio books.

www.AcesEbooks.com

Introduction

I want to thank you and congratulate you for buying the book, "Inspiration: Harnessing The Power Of Inspiration For True Greatness."

Do you feel like your life could use more inspiration? Are you looking for ways that will help you to get motivated so that you can take massive action towards your life goals? Is your true potential waiting to become unlocked? Understanding inspiration and feeling inspirational are two great ways to help you achieve all of your life dreams and more. When used properly, inspiration can be a powerful force that can help determine where you are headed in life. Inspiration can be a motivating force that allows you to bring out the best in yourself and live with the highest levels of self-confidence to make powerful changes in the world.

Over the last few hundred years there have been many inspirational people who have been able to focus their time and energy in order to achieve truly incredible things. Now, you can discover how to utilize the power of inspiration to motivate yourself to levels of greatness you may not of even thought possible. After reading this book, you too, can have the potential to leave a lasting impact on this world. Do you want to leave a legacy that lasts for decades to come? Be sure to use the tips and strategies in this book to get started on your own personal journey towards greatness!

This book contains proven steps and strategies on how to live a more inspirational life. After reading the information provided in this book, you can implement something from each chapter in your life to help unlock your hidden potential. You will learn a little more about inspiration and how it works. You will also learn about some daily habits that you can make a part of your life to become and feel more inspiring. Have you ever questioned your actions and why you do some things that you know isn't ideal? In this book, you will learn about how effective and properly implemented strategies can work wonders if done consistently over long periods of time. You will also learn about some real-life, inspiring people and how they have already made lasting changes in the world. Best of all, you will get the opportunity to practice some exercises to help you get more out of your life. Finally, you will read some of the all-time, best inspirational quotes that have been passed down for generations. You can refer to them at any time to get that extra boost of energy to start action on your goals and dreams!

Now, get ready to change your life! Head over to Chapter 1 and get ready to feel the inspiration!

Chapter 1: An Overview of Inspiration

Throughout your life, you have probably heard a lot about inspiration. Maybe you watched an inspirational video or heard an inspirational speech. Maybe you saw something that inspired you to take action, like seeing someone in a nice car or with a fit and healthy body. However, many people don't know the exact definition of inspiration. Inspiration is an invisible force that causes people to take action. Each person will tend to be inspired in different ways, and it is usually a desire to improve their life, their world, or something in it. Have you ever experienced an act of kindness and then felt inspired to pay it forward? Have you ever watched a documentary about those who are less fortunate than you and felt inspired to raise awareness about it? Have you ever watched an incredible physical feat on TV and felt inspired to improve yourself? The basic dictionary definition of inspiration is just a look at it on the surface. There are many underlying factors and questions to inspiration, one of the most popular being, "What inspires people? Why do people do what they do?"

Some believe that people become inspired to do things when they are trying to obtain a specific incentive—for example, some people may be inspired to lose weight to get a better-looking body. However, there is another side to looking at why people take certain actions. Some believe that inspiration is biological—in other words, humans are naturally inspired. For example, in 1949, a psychology professor named Harry Harlow conducted an experiment to measure the behavior of primates. During the experiment, a simple mechanical puzzle was presented to eight monkeys. Harlow used monkeys as his subjects because primates are the closest descendants to humans. The research team found that each monkey became interested in the puzzle without cause and immediately focused on learning how to solve it. At the end of the experiment, the monkeys were able to solve the puzzle in under a minute. When the team presented each monkey with an incentive, such as food, the monkey's desire in solving the puzzle declined.

This experiment led Harlow to believe that some people do not need an incentive to take action on something because the joy of carrying out the task was enough of a reward. So, in other words, inspiration can occur even when there is no solid incentive. A good way to view this is to look at one's job and one's free time. When you're at work, concrete incentives such as a raise or a new office are often the basis of inspiration to work harder. On the other hand, when you think about people who do things for no incentive, Harlow's theory about inspiration being biological makes sense as well. For example, think about volunteer first responders. They risk their lives and get no pay for helping others but there is a volunteer first aid squad or fire department in almost every community. If they don't get paid, then why do they do it?

Inspiration is a great thing to feel in the world today. Inspiration pushes people to be their best, it spreads a good vibe, and it can help you to transform yourself into a leader. Being able to feel inspired can help you keep your head up during dark times and it can help lead you to your life's purpose. Inspiration can be the driving factor in some of your biggest, life-altering decisions. Best of all, inspiration just happens. It cannot be bought or sold. It cannot be touched...but it's there, if you nourish it and want it to be. This book will take you through an exciting journey to learn how to better understand inspiration and how to utilize its incredible powers. So let's get started with one of the basic principles for nurturing inspiration in your daily life, the power of why.

Chapter 2: The Power of Why

In Chapter 1, you read about Professor Harlow's experiment with the monkeys as well as speculated on "why" people do the things they do, with or without a tangible reward. The power of asking the question "why" is a huge motivator for becoming inspirational. Many people do not need a tangible award to find satisfaction. Often times, they become inspired to do something just for the enjoyment it brings them or others.

For example, if you asked yourself, "*Why* do I workout hard?" your answer may be, "Because I want to look great in my bathing suit." Why do you work two jobs? "Because I love my kids and want to give them the best life possible." Remember in Chapter 1, how I rhetorically asked why people become volunteer first responders? Maybe it is because they lost a friend or a family member to an emergency and wanted to become an EMT to help prevent others from experiencing that. Whenever you ask "why" you want to do something, it should be followed with an answer that starts with, "Because..."

Asking the question "why?" can be a very powerful strategy in almost every aspect of your life and career. When you were a young child, you probably asked your parents, "why?" many times. It was because you wanted to better understand how things worked. However, learning is never-ending, and even as an adult, you can still use the question "why?" to gain a deeper understanding of how things work. By gaining a deeper understanding of how things work, your chances of feeling more inspired to move towards your goals will likely be much higher.

Asking the question "why?" is how many people end up making changes in themselves and in the world. This is usually because asking "why?" can lead you to the root cause of a problem. When you know the root cause of a problem, you can work on fixing it. I know this can sound a little confusing, so I will use a specific example to try and make this a bit clearer.

Let's say that you had a great idea...a solution to a worldwide problem. It could help people for years. However, to get that idea out to the world, you would have to put yourself out there and push it. While this may not be hard for some people, it could be much more difficult if you have a strong fear of failure or if you dread speaking in public. So, if you were to allow your fear of public speaking to overcome you, then it is likely your idea wouldn't make it very far and not too many lives would change. By simply asking yourself, "Why am I fearful of public speaking?" you can figure out the root cause—it may of been a bad experience that happened to you when you were younger. Common bad experiences in public speaking include getting teased by classmates or getting reprimanded by your teacher while you spoke in front of everybody.

Once you've figured out the root cause of your fear of public speaking, you will then be more aware of it and you can take steps to fix it. You can learn how to improve your public speaking skills and self-confidence until you're ready to face large audiences. Now, if you hadn't asked yourself, "Why am I fearful of public speaking?" then you may have never been able to overcome your fear and get your great ideas out to the world. Do you now have a better understanding of how powerful the question of "why?" can be?

Asking "why?" about almost anything can be effective. It doesn't just have to be about fears. When thinking about your future and your goals, ask yourself why you want to accomplish that goal. The answer to this question can serve as your main motivator and inspire you to work towards that goal each day. For example, if you want to be in great shape, ask yourself why. If the answer is so that you would feel confident enough to ask that special someone on a date, then be sure that you are thinking of this each day in the gym as you are steadily getting better and better.

When thinking about your past, ask yourself why you felt a certain way and then learn from that experience. When making a decision in the present moment, ask yourself why you would pick one route over the other. By taking a few moments to ask yourself this one word question, you can master a very powerful, yet simple, tool. Once you have the answer, be sure to write it down and remind yourself of it often. Use it as fuel to keep you inspired to keep moving towards your goal.

Chapter 3: Inspirational Habits

Though your everyday habits may seem small and insignificant, they are actually vitally important. When you have a variety of bad habits, the chances of your life going smoothly and happily is much more difficult. What you do every day, repeatedly, helps dictate how your future will turn out. Think about it for a moment—successful people tend to have the same types of habits and those who haven't really been successful in life also tend to share a lot of the same habits. When it comes to feeling inspirational and being inspirational, there are some very powerful habits that can help keep you feeling mentally strong and inspired. This chapter will explore some of the very best habits for becoming and staying inspired. Try replacing some of your bad habits with some of the good ones below and you are likely to see a dramatic improvement in your everyday life.

Some Of The Best Inspirational Habits

Don't Think About Materialism. Throughout life, it can be easy to get caught up in the world of commercialism or materialism—that is, focusing more on what physical things you can get (money, clothes, jewelry, cars, the latest electronics, etc). Get into the mindset that it is better to give and live in the present moment, rather than to try and get all of the assets that you can. By getting into this habit, you can see just how great life can be without having the latest popular sneakers or the latest handbag. You can focus more on finding ways to tackle real-life issues for both yourself and others. A great strategy for doing this is to make a list of all the things that you are currently grateful for in your life. You may be surprised at just how abundant you truly are and this can allow you to spend your precious mental power on more important matters instead of being envious, jealous, or always wanting something more.

Be Unique and Different. A great poem once spoke of a person picking one of two paths to walk down and the person picked the path that was obviously not traveled by many people, and then later he went on to say that it was a great choice. Be like the person in that poem and be brave. Be courageous. Dare to be different and do things that other people typically wouldn't do (positive, legal things, of course!). You never know what kind of impact you can have on the world just by doing something different than everybody else. Although it can sometimes feel like people look at you differently when you're unique, many people often secretly admire your ability to be unique.

Focus on Values, Be Successful. Get into the habit of focusing on your core values. Some of the most common values that people hold dear are their families, their religion, and their morals. Most of the time, your values are enough to inspire you to accomplish great things. For example, you might be inspired to start your own business because your parents struggled with hourly jobs and you do not want to provide that kind of life for your family. As long as your actions reflect your values, your chances of success will be greater.

Take Risks. Unless you take risks in your life, you may miss out on some of the best opportunities. In other words, you don't know if you will succeed at something unless you try. That way, if you do fail, you will know that you gave it your all and you will have a better chance at feeling inspired to try something else. Want to help the less fortunate? Do it! Want to apply for your dream job? Do it! Never give up! Many times in life, the most successful people aren't the smartest or the most qualified, they are the ones brave enough to take a risk and go for their dreams.

Think Positive. Positive thoughts can help you take action whenever you feel inspired. They also leave you in a better position to recognize and capitalize on good opportunities. If your head is filled with too many negative thoughts, your ability to be inspirational and actionable can severely decline. While it is definitely not always easy to do this, here are some good steps to take to get you thinking positively. Positive affirmations are excellent for combatting negative thoughts. Come up with empowering phrases and repeat it over and over in your head. Over time, these positive phrases can override much of the negative thoughts pop up in all of us from time to time. An example of a good positive affirmation is: "I am strong, happy, healthy, and loving life!" Another good idea is to limit your exposure to negative people. Try and surround yourself with positive and uplifting people and you may be surprised at how much happier and inspired you can be.

Watch Your Reactions. How you react to people, events, and circumstances can have a dramatic effect on your life. Your reactions generally reflect your attitude, which is usually a reflection on your actions and decisions. Although it can be difficult, if you can learn not to over react when things don't go the way you want them to, it will help you out much more in the long term. For example, if you react badly to a piece of criticism by your boss, you will likely not get as far as you would if you had reacted in a positive light, ready to make positive changes in your work ethic.

Be Reliable and Trustworthy. Show up to your commitments and go through with the things you say. This can help you stay on top of your game, whether at home or at work. For example, if you say you're going to start a fundraiser, do it, go through with it. When you take immediate action, you are more likely to complete your task and future tasks. Doing this also helps you become more credible and reliable to others—and that can often bring you much more opportunities. People who can be relied upon and trusted are greatly revered in society, and those who get through life by lying, making excuses, and performing poorly are generally looked down upon and disliked.

Stick to Your Passions and Talents. Have you ever put one of your talents or passions on the back-burner because it wasn't "practical" or a good career path? The fear of failure or of being judged harshly has led many people to follow a path that has made them miserable. The happiest people in life are those who are able to make a living by following their passion. It doesn't matter what others say, it's your life. Even if it takes you decades, being able to find your passion and live a fulfilling life is priceless. When you are following your passion, you are no longer working; you are living at your true potential and inspiration will naturally follow you wherever you go.

Never Verbally Berate Others. People often forget things you say or do but very rarely do people forget it if you hurt their feelings. With bullying and cyber bullying on the rise in today's world, even between adults, you can make a difference by saying kind things to others. By doing this, you can also inspire others to do the same and you are much more likely to have things go your way with that person in the future if needed. There was once a story about a man who walked his way to a bridge and jumped off it. Later on, his family found a suicide note that said, he would have turned around if one person smiled at him on his way to the bridge. I don't know how true that story is, but it is a great example of how one small kind gesture can change the life of a stranger.

Take the Reins of Your Life. It is easy to let yourself get caught up in your daily responsibilities, so much so that your life begins to take charge of you. Turn it the other way around and take charge of your life. You control your destiny and all the good things that come from it by doing the right things. By knowing what works best for you and making a strategic plan for doing them effectively, you can get so much more done and be much more effective. For more detailed help in this matter, be sure to check out my book: Influence, Willpower, and Discipline.

Overcome Fear. To accomplish almost anything big, you must overcome your fears. Fear can hold you back from many things. Identify the fog of fear that is holding you back and clear it from your life. Once you master how to overcome fear, you can feel more inspired to take more risks and try new things. Learning how to overcome fear can also help you boost your self-confidence and motivation. For more information on defeating fear in your life, check out my bestselling book: Overcoming Fear.

Forgiveness and Keeping the Past in the Past. If you focus too much on your past and not you're present, the chances of you creating a better future for yourself can go down dramatically. What you do in the present directly affects where you end up in the future. If you must focus on the past, allow it to inspire you to improve. However, if your past is in front of you, you will keep going in circles. Be sure to utilize the healing power of forgiveness to allow this to happen. Everyone has anger, resentment, hatred, and other unhealthy emotions that do nothing towards adding real value to your life. By allowing yourself to forgive the people or circumstances in the past that cause these emotions to surface, you can instead focus on more positive and uplifting things that can help move yourself forward. It is also much easier to feel inspired when you are in a positive frame of mind than when you are angry and frustrated about things that happened months, years, or even decades ago. If you would like more help in letting go of things from the past, be sure to check out my book on Forgiveness.

Appreciate Your Challenges. Make it a habit to look at your challenges and struggles in a positive light—they brought you to where you are now. Anticipate your future challenges and struggles as things that will help you learn and grow. Whenever you're feeling discouraged, remind yourself of a previous challenge that you overcame and in what ways it positively affected your life—this can help you get through the next challenge. It is also a good idea to have a success journal. In this journal you can write down all of the great accomplishments and things that happened throughout your life. By reading this journal daily, you will feel inspired to tackle your goals with renewed strength and ferocity. I also personally like to put these successes on a voice recorder and then play them back whenever I like. You may be surprised at how many incredible things you have done throughout your life that don't easily pop back into your head without these nice little reminders.

Help Others. By giving others a hand when they are down or out, you can feel good about yourself. It also builds up good karma and is great for your reputation. Also, many people like to pay good deeds forward which have all sorts of positive unintended consequences. After you feel how good it is to help others, you will be more likely to do it again in the future.

Be the Change. One of the best inspirational habit to get into is to be the change that you want to make. Don't wait around for it to happen because you don't know if it actually will. Take the action necessary to make the change. Also, when becoming the change you want to see, aim for the biggest impact possible. Think of it this way—if you have a loved one who suffers from a disease without a cure, don't just try to raise awareness on the local level...try as hard as you can to raise awareness on the global level. That way, you start a trend, and not only will you be helping your loved one but you will be helping other peoples' loved ones at the same time. By learning how to work together on a global scale, you can make great changes that will have a positive impact on lives for years.

Inspirational Reading, Music, and Pictures. It isn't always easy to feel inspired and it is very tough to make it come on demand. You can greatly increase your chances of becoming inspired by regularly reading inspirational quotes, stories, biographies or literature. Music is also an incredible motivating force! Be sure to collect the music that makes you feel good and that inspires you towards action. One of my favorite things to do is to make my own music play lists comprised of all my favorite motivational and inspirational songs. By listening to inspirational music daily, you greatly increase your chances of being inspired to accomplish your goals in life. Finally, beautiful artwork and pictures can be very inspiring. I have beautiful artwork all over my house and a variety of books filled with all sorts of magnificent pictures. One of my favorite things to do is to cut out my favorite pictures, put them on poster board, frame it, and hang it on the wall. Old calendars and picture books are great for this. I also do the same for my own personal books of favorite pictures. If I see a great picture in a magazine, online, or anywhere I else, I simply print it out or cut it out and then add it to my own personal picture book. Try listening to your favorite music while looking at your favorite pictures for a really good boost.

For more great habits, be sure to check out my bestselling book: The Top 100 Best Habits.

Chapter 4: Inspiring People/Stories

If you were to open a basic history book, you would most likely read about many people who have changed the world through their actions, their stories, their determination, and their accomplishments. If it were not for many of the most famous historical figures, you would be living in a completely different world today. This chapter will take a look at some of the best inspirational role models in history and how their actions have created the world you live in today. You will also have the chance to watch some inspirational videos about people who are currently taking steps to change themselves and the world. Knowing that people have done things in the past and are still making efforts today is inspiring in itself. Will you be one of those people who will go down in history as well?

Martin Luther King. Martin Luther King is known as of the most famous civil rights activists in the history of the United States. He led nonviolent and peaceful protests to help end the segregation of white people and African Americans. He assisted in organizing the Montgomery Bus Boycott in which African Americans refused to use the bus services due to segregated seating. In turn, this sparked the Supreme Court to rule segregated seating as unconstitutional. He also made many inspirational speeches that focused on changing the future, rather than wallowing in the troubles of the past and present. He was awarded the Nobel Peace Prize and was later assassinated. Today, there is a holiday in his honor. Martin Luther King is an inspirational person because he served as the symbol of justice for ending racism and bringing people of all skin colors together. If it were not for King, the world may very well be a different place today. Instead, he inspired people to stand up for their rights and to view others as equals.

Albert Einstein. Albert Einstein is best known as the genius of the twentieth century who made amazing theories in physics, but what many people do not know is that Einstein was not always regarded as a genius. Einstein did not learn how to speak for an usually longer time than those of his age and his teachers viewed him as slow and dimwitted. By the time he was a teenager, he became fascinated in mathematics and began to teach much of it to himself. He went on to teach math and physics to others. Outside of his studies, he stood up for many American civil rights movements, such as the movement to end lynching. Despite his level of formal education, Einstein is an inspirational person because he was able to make a difference in the technical world. He studied math because he enjoyed it and eventually came up with some of the best known theories, like the Quantum Theory and the Theory of Relativity. Without Einstein and his works, the world of science and physics would not have evolved as quickly as it did.

William Shakespeare. William Shakespeare is one of the most well-known names in the history of English literature. Although the details of his life are scarce and up in the air, there is no doubt that Shakespeare wrote some of the best poems, sonnets, comedies, and tragedies in all of literature. His plays have been studies for years. Shakespeare is an inspirational figure in English literature. Even today, many modern stories use Shakespeare's plays as a foundation. His plays have touched on issues that are still relevant today, such as interracial dating and forbidden love. His plays have inspired movies, shows, and new ideas throughout the last several centuries. His works have inspired many writers and artists and will most likely continue to inspire them for many years to come.

Susan B. Anthony. Susan B. Anthony is a well-known, inspirational figure from the early 1800s who spoke out against slavery and in favor of women's rights. Originally raised as a Quaker, Susan B. Anthony excelled at education, despite the fact that few women were educated at the time. Her father helped her learn math and she became a teacher. While she was a teacher, she felt that women were paid less than men and decided to do something about it. She was able to fight for a woman's right to vote and wrote a publication that argued for better pay. She believed that women and African Americans deserved the same rights as men. Fourteen years after she died, the 19th amendment to the Constitution ensured women's rights to vote. Susan B. Anthony is an inspirational figure for those who desire to fight for what is right and just in the world. Although there are still some issues with women still getting paid less than men to work, there are modern activists who are working to end that, too. Susan B. Anthony was one of the first women to spark that fight.

Mother Teresa. Mother Teresa, another recipient of the Nobel Peace Prize, was a Roman Catholic nun who fought for and served poor people all around the world. As a nun, she did most of her work in India where she helped the poor and lived as a poor person herself. However, she was eventually able to open a home where neglected people could die peacefully, by her side. She was then able to extend her services to orphans and the terminally ill on a global scale. She also stood by her views on abortions, divorces, and the death penalty, even though many people disagreed with her opinion. As she grew older, she endured several health issues, but never stopped caring about others. She donated the money from the Nobel Peace Prize to those who were in need. Mother Teresa is an inspirational person because she dedicated her life to helping people who had nobody else. She is a great role model for standing strong for those in need and she is also a perfect example of how helping people on a global scale can make a great impact on the world.

Eleanor Roosevelt. Eleanor Roosevelt, wife of former president Franklin D. Roosevelt is another inspirational woman in American history. She was one of the first Ladies to speak publicly and often spoke to those who were unemployed during the Great Depression. For women, she served as a role model because she did not live the traditional domestic life. During World War II, she helped motivate and encourage the soldiers in the Pacific by speaking to them. She encouraged African Americans to take more visible roles in the military and further advocated for more African American rights. After World War II, she was appointed to the United Nations General Assembly, where she was able to help write the Declaration of Humans Rights. Eleanor Roosevelt is an inspiration for women in politics, independent women, and for racial equality.

Inspirational Role Models of Today

Tony Robbins. One of the best inspirational role models of the modern era is Anthony Robbins. I have been listening to his motivational tapes and cd's for nearly two decades. He is someone who has dedicated his life to finding the best strategies and techniques for personal development and success. Even after he has become a multi-millionaire with plenty of money to live his life doing whatever he wants, he continues to push forward, eat healthy, exercise, do seminars, discover new techniques, and live life to the fullest. I would definitely recommend Tony's get the edge series to anyone looking to take their life to the next level. Here is a great YouTube video: Tony Robbins explains how to focus by OwnYourReality.

Randy Paush, a professor at Carnegie Mellon University who was diagnosed with pancreatic cancer, gives a graduation speech to the class of 2008, noting the importance of living a fulfilling life before it is too late. Check out his speech in this Youtube Video posted by JohnNada80, Dying College Professor Gives Inspiring Speech.

Arnold Schwarzenegger. Arnold is another inspiring figure. He came to America with nearly nothing and ended up being a 6 time Mr. Olympia, one of the greatest movie action stars of all time, and the governor of California. I think one of the main reasons people really like Arnold is because of his work ethic. When he does a movie or competition, he is giving it his all! He is doing everything possible to succeed and busting his butt to do so! He doesn't just coast along like many others, he is putting in the effort, day in and day out to succeed, and that is truly an admirable quality. Here is one of my favorite YouTube videos of Arnold's Six Secrets To Success posted by Travis Fisher.

Some Other Inspirational YouTube videos

I am a Champion by Pawel Jedrzejak
Dare To Be Great by Safin de Zane
How Great I am posted by mbm34
The Difference Between A Winner And A Loser posted by Refpeople

Chapter 5: Your Inspirational Action Plan

Now that you have come this far in learning about inspiration, how to nurture inspiration in your life, and discovered how other people have made inspirational impacts in the world, it is time to start working on your own ability to inspire and be inspirational to others. This chapter contains 5 interactive exercises that you can practice to help build your self-confidence and determination to live a more inspiring life. I tried to include an exercise for everybody—you can try all 5 or you can pick and choose the ones that you are most comfortable with. All in all, I hope they are able to help you develop your inspirational abilities even further!

Exercise #1: The Imagination Exercise

Imagine that you had a twin. Your twin is in your house or your office, working on a project, one that you've been working on for quite a while. Upon closer inspection, you find that your twin is working three times as hard you have been. Just by being next to your twin, you can sense his or her strengths, hitting you like a truck. All you say is, "Wow!" Looking at your twin closer, you notice a tall posture, a look of determination in the eyes, and you feel an amazing energy. Your twin turns and it looks like he or she stares at you but what they really have is a certain, strong confidence in the eyes. Your twin looks focused.

At that moment, you realize that what you're looking at isn't a human—you're looking at greatness, in the form of yourself. The greatness is so powerful that it feels like you're standing next to a super human. You then realize, that your twin is not a super human, or anybody else—it's you. Deep down inside, you know that you can unlock that greatness within yourself. Why aren't you that person right now?

The only thing that's holding you back is FEAR. Once you overcome whatever fears you have, you can be that person for the rest of your life. Don't delay it and don't hesitate—go do something today that will get you one step closer. Be sure to do this visualization daily.

Exercise #2: Inspiration Through Visualization

To achieve your goals and your dreams, it is essential to visualize yourself doing it. Visualization is a very powerful technique that can boost your feelings of inspiration to get there. Let's look at a famous example to see just how powerful and inspiring visualization can be—Jim Carrey, the actor, used to park his car in famous spots in California to feel what his life could be like if he made it big. He even wrote himself a huge check and dated it 5 years from then. Right around the time he dated the check, he was paid $10,000,000 to be in the movie *Dumb and Dumber*.

If visualization could inspire somebody like Jim Carrey to do great things in his life, imagine what it could help you do in *your* life! Still not convinced? Leave it to science—your brain is programmed in a way in which it cannot tell the difference between reality and a projected reality. That means that visualization is a proven technique for reaching your goals. This exercise aims to help you make the most of the visualization technique.

The first thing you should do is to include all of your senses in your vision. Imagine what you'll hear, imagine what you'll touch, and imagine what you'll taste. Even think about what you'll smell. Picture how you will celebrate great things, how you'll laugh, smile, celebrate, or anything else. Really submerge yourself in your vision. Make it as real as possible.

The second thing you should do is visualize your accomplishments from different angles. See yourself as if you were in a movie and you are the lead role. Picture yourself reaching your dreams from your own eyes and then picture how others will see it. Picture it as if you were reading a book written about yourself in the third-person. If you can think of any other eyes to picture it from, do it.

The third thing you should do is to start to live your goals and dreams as much as you can. Dress how you would dress if you were an entrepreneur and act as you would act if you were a doctor. If you want to be a motivational speaker, start thinking and acting like one. Whatever you want to do, start living and acting like you already do it. Live your life so that you give off a vibe of who you eventually want to be known as.

The fourth thing you should do is pair affirmations with your mental images. Say things to yourself that you can imagine others saying about you once you've made it. Create your positive affirmations from different view points, just as you did with your visualizations.

Finally, the fifth thing you should do is make a physical visual. One good idea is to put together a collage of your dreams. You could hang up inspirational quotes in your workspace, you could use pictures, and you could put together videos. You could do anything that works for you, as long as it reminds you daily about working toward your visions and goals. For this to be successful, you need to do it daily or multiple times per day. Just doing it a few times or once a week just isn't going to be enough to get the full desired results.

Exercise #3: Boosting Your Self-Confidence

Without a strong sense of self-confidence, it is likely that you will not even be able to fully utilize the powerful feeling of inspiration to get where you want to be. Remember how confident your twin was in the imagination exercise? Knowing how to become that confident is crucial for inspiring yourself and others. Many people experience a period of low self-confidence at various points in their lives, but the good news is that this is only temporary. Everybody has a life purpose and can find a variety of reasons to hold their heads high.

When depressed, people find that it is very hard, almost impossible, to boost their self-confidence. However, by using the right techniques and strategies, anyone can boost their self-confidence. It can be very easy to practice boosting your own self-confidence. The better you get at it, and the more confident you will feel, and the more likely you will feel inspired to do things. This exercise aims to help you identify the signs of low self-confidence and learn how to make the necessary changes.

Do You…   **How to Fix It…**

Do You…	How to Fix It…
Check your phone during social interactions?	Start going out by yourself. Don't distract yourself with your phone. Once you get comfortable being alone, you'll feel more comfortable being alone with others.
Spend too much time trying to make yourself look perfect before you leave home?	Ask yourself how you really want to look and focus on making it happen. Wear what people you want to be like wear. You'll be able to look at yourself and feel great.
Go out of your way to avoid conflict?	Every time you feel yourself bending the truth to avoid conflict, try to think of a better way to tell the truth, without confronting or being aggressive.
Have an addiction to try to offset stress? (Includes anything, not just drugs)	Any time you feel the need to engage in your addiction, exert some willpower to stop yourself and then later on say, "I survived." Do this continuously.
Try to assume what other people are thinking?	Every time you try to assume what a person is thinking of, stop and consider that they may be thinking the opposite. Then, simply ask them what they're thinking.

These are just a few of the most common signs of low self-confidence. For more interaction, try to identify your own signs and brainstorm what you can do to fix them based off these few examples.

Some other great ways to boost confidence include strength training, Hypnosis, Exercise, constantly working to improve yourself, reading positive books on things you would like to improve upon, taking action towards overcoming your fears and surrounding yourself with good friends and family members. When you are strong and healthy, everything else falls into place much easier. If you would more information on getting yourself as healthy as you can possibly be, be sure to check out my bestselling book: Ultimate Health Secrets. To bring your confidence to a whole new level, then check out my book on Confidence.

Exercise #4: Experiencing Spirituality and Religion

Many people become inspired through their religion. Not everybody practices the same religions or practices one at all, and not everybody is spiritual, but if one of these two principles apply to you, then feel free to check out this exercise. Religion and spirituality tend to help people become inspired because they have the ability to fill an emptiness that may be in their life. Spirituality helps many people differentiate between feeling wealthy from money and from feeling wealthy with inner-happiness. If you believe that religion or spirituality can help you become more inspired and fulfilled, try out some of the following things.

Give Back. Many people misinterpret the meaning of success. While some believe that being successful is having everything you've ever wanted, being successful can also include giving things away to others. Many large, successful companies practice this value. Think about the last time you went out to eat and your host asked you to donate a dollar to the latest world tragedy. Not only does giving back give you a sense of fulfillment in helping others out, but it also creates a wave of inspiration all around. Others will be more likely to view you as caring and humanistic, which could even help you get more business and make new connections.

Cause and Effect. When you interact with somebody, not only are you affecting him or her but you're also affecting his or her family and friends. This is kind of like the rule that says treat others the way you'd want them to treat you. Others like to call it Karma. By treating people well, you can spiritually send a wave of goodness to all of their contacts, who may then pass it on to others as well. This is an activity that can help you feel good about yourself and it also makes you look great to others, who may have opportunities for you.

Explore Your Life Purpose. A common belief is that everyone is born with a life purpose. Everyone is born with certain talents and gifts as well as strengths and weaknesses. If you take a few moments to write out your strengths, weaknesses, talents, and gifts and how you can use them in a positive light, not only will you be practicing visualization but you will be actively encouraging yourself and taking one step further toward your dreams.

Exercise# 5: Learn From Others

What is one of the most effective ways to learn? It's to learn from the actions of others. Most of us have learned this way. Maybe you grew up watching your older siblings get in trouble for things and you learned not to repeat the same actions. Maybe you learned your work ethic from all of your parents' hard work. However it's happened, you have most likely learned something key from somebody at some point in your life. Learning from others is probably the biggest key in all of inspiration—after all, isn't that what inspiring people is all about?

To really feel inspired and to bring out the best in yourself, a great idea is to find a mentor. Just because you've grown up doesn't mean you can't stop learning from others. A mentor can show you what to do, how to act, how to dress, and anything else you need to know for success. The best kind of mentor to have is somebody who is already in a position that you want to be in one day. So, if you want to eventually become an accountant, find somebody who is already experienced in the accounting/finance area and ask them to be your mentor. Having a mentor can teach you a lot, which in turn can help you feel really inspired to actually become one. Great ways to find mentors are to use Social Media groups, attend local seminars, or to just simply ask somebody. Your mentor does not have to be anyone famous—just somebody who is willing to show you the ropes or keep you accountable. Another new name for mentors is a life coach. Take five minutes and think about anyone that you already know who may be willing to mentor you. Shoot them an email or give them a quick phone call—remember, you'll never know unless you ask. If they say no, don't give up—keeping looking! Many of the greatest people in the world went on to great success because of the help of a mentor. If you can't find a mentor or may find them a bit expensive, a good investment is in Tony Robbins audio cd's, he does a great job.

Chapter 6: Inspirational Quotes

Working on living an inspirational life can be challenging at times, and often times it can even get a little discouraging. Whenever you are feeling like you can't accomplish your goals, reach your dreams, or inspire yourself or others, refer to some of the great inspirational quotes in this chapter. Each one is packed with excellent wisdom and knowledge that can help you pick yourself up and keep going strong.

Inspirational Quotes

"A goal is a dream with a deadline" – Napoleon Hill

"Shoot for the moon. Even if you miss, you'll land among the stars" – Les Brown

"A winner is someone who recognizes his God given talents, works his tail off to develop them into skills, and uses these skills to accomplish his goals" – Larry Bird

"A good plan today is better than a great plan tomorrow" – George S. Patton

"Celebrate any progress. Don't wait to get perfect" – Ann McGee Cooper

"What the mind can conceive and believe, it can achieve" – Napoleon Hill

"Use the losses and failures of the past as a reason for action, not inaction" – Charles J. Givens

"Each one of us has a fire in our heart for something. It's our goal in life to find it and keep it lit" – Mary Lou Retton

"The discipline you learn and character you build from setting and achieving a goal can be more valuable than the achievement of the goal itself" – Bo Bennett

"Put your future in good hands. Your own" – Mark Victor Hansen

"If you don't know where you are going, you'll end up someplace else" – Yogi Berra

"Those who do not create the future they want must endure the future they get" – Draper L. Kaufman, Jr.

"If you don't like what you're doing, then don't do it" – Ray Bradbury

"Great minds have purposes, others have wishes" – Washington Irving

"Decide on what you think is right, and stick to it" – George Eliot

"To accomplish our destiny…we must cover before nightfall the distance assigned to each of us" – Dr. Alexis Carrel

"When your values are clear to you, making decisions becomes easier" – Roy Disney

"It is in the moment of our decisions that our destinies are created" – Anthony Robbins

"The more you listen to the voice within you, the better you will hear what is sounding outside" – Dag Hammarskjold

"Any time you're tempted to say, "Impossible", add an apostrophe and a space, and say, "I'm possible"" - Al Secunda

"Live up to your potential instead of living up to someone else's" – Martha Burgess

"You're either part of the solution or you're part of the problem" – Eldridge Cleaver

"Fear paralyzes; curiosity empowers. Be more interested than afraid" – Patricia Alexander

"Sooner or later, those who win are those who think they can" – Richard Bach

"If you change your thinking, you can change your life" – Brian Tracy

"Most of us have far more courage than we ever dreamed we possessed" – Dale Carnegie

"The gem cannot be polished without friction, nor man perfected without trials" – Chinese proverb

"Every really new idea looks crazy at first" – Abraham Maslow

"Knowledge is power. The more knowledge, expertise, and connections you have, the easier it is for you to make a profit at the game of your choice" – Stuart Wilde

"Time is our most valuable asset, yet we tend to waste it, kill it, and spend it rather than invest it" – Jim Rohn

"Your attitude, not your aptitude, will determine your altitude" – Zig Ziglar

"Believing in yourself is an endless destination. Believing you have failed, is the end of your journey" – Sarah Meredith

"What we have done for ourselves alone dies with us. What we have done for others and the world remains and is immortal" – Albert Pine

"Catch people in the act of doing something right" – Ken Blanchard

"Never miss an opportunity to make someone smile" – Unknown

"To serve is beautiful, but only if it is done with joy and a whole heart and a free mind" – Pearl S. Buck

Conclusion

I hope this book was able to help you bring more inspiration into your life now and for many years to come.

The next step is to use the inspiration that is burning in your heart to accomplish your goals and dreams. Be sure to use everything you have learned in this book to daily do what is needed to keep the fires of motivation burning strong. And most important of all... when you feel inspired... Act Immediately! Be sure to practice the exercises from Chapter 5 daily and to feed your brain with positive thoughts, music, affirmations, books, and pictures as much as possible. You don't have to try and make a difference on a global scale just yet—start small and try to make a difference in your life and another person's life. Once you see how powerful and great the force of inspiration can be, continue to practice it until you are able to make a lasting impact on the world!

Finally, if you discovered at least one thing that has helped you or that you think would be beneficial to someone else, be sure to take a few seconds to easily post a quick positive review. As an author, your positive feedback is desperately needed. Your highly valuable five star reviews are like a river of golden joy flowing through a sunny forest of mighty trees and beautiful flowers! *To do your good deed in making the world a better place by helping others with your valuable insight, just leave a nice review.*

My Other Books and Audio Books
www.AcesEbooks.com

Peak Performance Books

Health Books

Be sure to check out my audio books as well!

 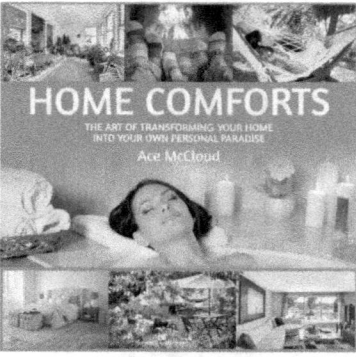 

Check out my website at: **www.AcesEbooks.com** for a complete list of all of my books and high quality audio books. I enjoy bringing you the best knowledge in the world and wish you the best in using this information to make your journey through life better and more enjoyable! **Best of luck to you!**

www.ingramcontent.com/pod-product-compliance
Lightning Source LLC
Chambersburg PA
CBHW051429070526
44584CB00023B/3651